A MANUAL ON

HOW TO DEAL

WITH A BULLY IN THE

WORKPLACE

Jan Marquart LCSW

Jan Marquart LCSW

www.JanMarquart.com

CEO - About the Author Network

jan_marquart@yahoo.com or
jan@AboutTheAuthorNetwork.com

USA

TABLE OF CONTENTS

Introduction

Having a bully in the workplace is a corporate disaster in companies all across the world. It is a significant contributor to the loss of productivity, good employees, and profit. This 'how to' manual is designed for victims of bullying in the workplace, employees, and management staff.

The writing of this manual did not come about because of a random study on the phenomenon of bullying in the workplace. This manual came about because there is no better time to speak out than when you have had enough of a needless problem in your own life.

When I started working in the corporate world in 1967 I was seventeen, adorable, and terribly naïve. Over the years I have been bullied in the workplace quite a few times as well as having been witness to others being bullied.

Unless the act of bullying involves one of the bulleted descriptions listed under *legal discriminations* as defined by the HUD office required to be posted on all office bulletin boards, getting help from a supervisor for a problem with bullying is rare. I've watched many good employees over the years quit jobs they were good at because the stress of a bully was more than they could handle. I've seen supervisors bully staff as well as employees who sought advancement become cruel in their efforts to do so to their co-workers. I have quit a couple of jobs because the dysfunction of bullies had everyone intimidated and going to work was like entering a war zone. Bullies are terrorists in the workplace. The chaos they cause in companies is tantamount to the dysfunction the alcoholic or seriously mentally ill cause in families.

Unless a department has management staff that is astute enough to identify that they have a bully in the office, the problem can become disastrous. For the most part, supervisors are trained to handle problems with customers – not bullying employees.

In 1982 I worked for an EAP program. Shortly after being employed I was asked to go into corporations and teach workshops. I spent a great deal of time listening to supervisors and their staffing teams complain about bullying situations.

At one point in my career I obtained a position with a great company. I loved the work and its mission and both enjoyed and respected the professionals with whom I worked. I was a happy camper. Then the company hired someone, who within a few days assaulted me. I went into my supervisor's office and described what happened. Later that day I spoke to her again, and the next day I took the matter to her supervisor. For the next three months matters accelerated. I went to a third supervisor up the hierarchical ladder, but nothing changed. I kept copies of emails and a completed Documentation Sheet on my home computer, just in case I needed it. I would have quit but I loved my job and the other people on my team.

For three months I begged the supervisors to meet with the two of us. Finally, my supervisor agreed to meet with us on a Monday - but the Friday before I was called into her office by her supervisor. She stood close to me, pointed her finger in my face, and screamed that all the problems in the department were my fault. She blamed me for putting notices around the office that dictated how everyone should behave even though I had not placed one notice anywhere. She added that when I gave her the mail it made a noise as it hit the desk and she didn't like that. She brought up the fact that months ago I sneezed at her perfume when at the time she had denied wearing any. The whole conversation was unreal, untrue, and out of focus. But I saw what was coming.

Being a supervisor is a serious position. Corporate offices spend a good deal of time and money on training staff to deal with making paying customers happy but not nearly enough time on employee relationships. Although there is no law on the books for generic bullying I have written this manual for the well-being of all involved. I hope this manual, which is brief and to the point, helps all parties.

Chapter I – The Law

The bad news: there is not one state in the Union that has a law on its books against generic bullying in the workplace.

The good news: it is only a matter of time before the victims of abusive-by bullying take a stand for a law against bullying.

Until that time occurs, I have written this manual to help. The internet is replete with sites for victims to post poetry and add to discussion blogs. Just Google: bullying in the workplace or poems about bullying in the workplace to see how many people around the world are troubled by this problem. I was stunned at how many sites I found.

Let's look at what is already on the books. The HUD equal employment opportunity requirements listed below are meant to prohibit discrimination against employees or applicants based on race, color, religion, sex, national origin, age, disability, or economic status, that apply to hiring practices, employer/employee relations, and business opportunity.

Examples of legal discriminatory practices in employment include the following:

1. harassment based on race, color, religion, sex, national origin, disability, or age,

2. retaliation against an individual for filing a charge of discrimination, participating in a discrimination investigation, or opposing discriminatory practices,

3. employment decisions based on stereotypes or assumptions about the abilities, traits, or performance

of individuals of a certain sex, race, age, religion, ethnic group, or any individual with a disability, and

4. denying employment opportunities to a person because of marriage to, or association with, an individual of a particular race, religion, national origin, or with a disability. Title VII also prohibits discrimination because of participation in schools or places of worship associated with a particular racial, ethnic, or religious group.

To get more detailed information there is an Equal Employment Opportunity Commission Website to review. http://www.eeoc.gov/laws/types/

Note: the above information is on the HUD website which is a fabulous website to find information on harassment issues. http://portal.hud.gov/hudportal/HUD.

Discrimination in the workplace came out of legislation that focused on discrimination in housing laws. This site is a good resource for getting historical information. http://portal.hud.gov/hudportal/HUD?src=/about/hud_history - this is the specific link for the history of discrimination laws.

In the hiring process employees receive a statement like the one above to sign along with other notifications of company policy. Each situation above involves an act of bullying yet there is nothing for the generic acts of bullying that can have an enormous effect on the health of employees and company productivity. How to handle this dilemma is described in the following chapters.

Chapter II – What is a Bully?

Let's examine what a bully is and reasons why he does what he does.

Simply put, a bully is an angry person who incites fear, intimidation, helplessness, powerlessness, and creates hostility into an environment, and he does so persistently.

A bully rarely apologizes or stops bullying behavior. The bully views his actions as appropriate due to some personal philosophy of revenge, power, and justice based on past experiences in his own life. He does not believe that he is doing anything wrong, and is too angry to either care or be able to view the effects of his behavior from another's perspective. In other words, there is little if any empathy or compassion.

Everyone has a bad day now and then but a healthy person understands his behavior and makes amends for it by apologizing or doing whatever else is required. Those who express a one-time bullying event are not the focus of this manual. (Note: The word 'he' is used, however, bullies can be women too.)

Persistent bullying leans towards sociopathic behavior and steps over social and polite customs with narcissistic self-motivated purposes. I use the word sociopathic because bullies do not usually have any regard for how other people feel or for what the rules of a civilized society are. What he does know are the experiences of helplessness, powerlessness, and of life spinning out of control which serves to cause his deep-rooted anger to seek justice, consciously or subconsciously. Underlying the behavior of any bully is long-time unresolved anger, loss, shame, and grief. The bully projects his own misery onto others because in his mind, by doing the same thing to others, he is evening out the score and restoring his sense of personal power. Although this mental paradigm is never met with success, a bully does not truly get this fact. They persist in the act of bullying because that is all they know. This way of behaving usually originated in childhood where abusive issues never got resolved, addressed, or worked out. Thus the patterns have continued into adulthood. This is one of the reasons why bullying behavior becomes a persistent pattern in the corporate family.

Bullies often have a narcissistic personality disorder. Everything has to go their way or they throw a tantrum. They will target an employee that they see as weak or afraid of speaking up. The bully will set up the situation so the employee he is picking on experiences the helplessness and powerlessness the bully once felt. Just like any other learning experience, bullies show us what they have learned. It is best not to try and counsel these clients in the workplace but rather give firm and clear guidelines for what is expected of them.

The psychology of a bully is nothing to mess with. Bullying in the workplace did not start in the workplace. Again, it started in childhood and is deep-rooted. I emphasize this so supervisors don't believe that they can change the mentality of a bully simply with an assertive or counseling type of voice in a meeting. The only thing that can be *re-organized* is the expected behavior and this expectation must be presented clearly in order to change the dysfunctional behavior, not the bully's attitude or way he sees the world. Supervisors should not try to get inside the bully's head.

[9]

Lean on company procedural manuals which should describe the expected behavior in the office. Remember: the only purpose here is to keep everyone safe.
I review this in more detail in Chapter IX. Look at it this way: bullying is a PTSD response to a long-term traumatic chain of events. Perhaps as a child the bully was physically, sexually, or emotionally abused with no freedom to speak up about their discomfort in the family. Now the bully is in your office. Just how much do you think you can resolve with someone with deep-rooted traumatic issues?

Luckily the work environment is regulated by a code of behavioral professionalism and supervisors are responsible, despite the lack of laws, to protect their employees from a hostile work environment. Unfortunately, many supervisors view bullying problems as personality conflicts. Nothing could be further from the truth. No victim of bullying should ever confront these individuals alone, even if the supervisor requests them to. No victim ought ever to have private meetings with them or isolate themselves with them in any way for any reason.

Being nice to a bully does not change them. Victims should leave them alone. These dysfunctional individuals are the responsibility of management.

Chapter III – Examples of Bullying in the Workplace

Here is a definition of bullying in the workplace.

> *Repeated* incidents forming a pattern of behavior, expressed through words or actions, intended to intimidate, offend, degrade, or humiliate a particular person or group of people.

The key word here is *repeated*. If some of these behaviors are happening to you or you are witnessing them happening to someone else – there is a problem with a bully in your office.

1. spreading malicious rumors, gossip, or innuendo that is not true
2. excluding or isolating someone from group interactions
3. being intimidating
4. undermining or deliberately impeding an employee's work
5. physically abusing or threatening to abuse
6. removing areas of responsibilities without giving a reason or having a purpose
7. repeatedly changing work guidelines
8. establishing impossible deadlines that sets up an employee to fail
9. withholding necessary information or purposefully giving wrongful information on a project
10. making jokes that are designed to offend or harm
11. spying, stalking, lurking, or in some other way, intruding an employee's privacy

12. creating helplessness by not giving an employee enough work to keep them busy
13. yelling or using profanity
14. persistently giving criticism
15. repeatedly belittling an employee's opinion
16. undeserved disciplinary action (administered by a bully supervisor)
17. blocking applications for promotion, training, or any type of advancement
18. tampering with an employee's work station, project, time sheet, or any other work-related item
19. belittling an employee in a group, such as meetings, conferences, social business events

Chapter IV – Astounding Statistics

In August 2010 two studies were conducted by the Workplace Bullying Institute to collect data on American adults. If you were not part of this study and you have been bullied, then the statistics are even higher.

Here is what the study revealed:

- 35% of workers have experienced bullying firsthand
- 62% of bullies are men
- 58% of targets are women
- women bullies target women in 80% of cases
- bullying at work is four times more prevalent than illegal harassment
- same-gender harassment accounts for more than 2/3 (68%) of bullying

In addition 15% stated they witnessed someone being bullied.

Note: These statistics were found at: www.workplacebullying.org/2010/09/30/workplace-bullying. Other astounding statistics can be found on this page.

In 2006 Schat, Frone & Kelloway did a survey and found that 41.4% of respondents to their survey reported experiencing psychological aggression at work. That represents 47 million US workers.

Bullying behavior also pertains to cyber-bullying which conforms to the behavior for generic bullying in this manual. The following statistical information was found on http://www.northeastern.edu/securenu/?p=1995.

A new study by the University of Sheffield and Nottingham University has shown that 8 out of 10 people have experienced cyber-bullying at the workplace in the last six months. The research also has shown that 14-20 percent of people felt they [had] been [a] victim of cyber-bullying at least once a week.

Chapter V – Signs that Indicate a Bully Might Be the Problem

Supervisors should take note when the following situations are present:

- increased absenteeism
- increased turnover of staff
- increased stress in getting staff to respond to their requests
- increased costs due to EAP counseling sessions in a certain department
- increased accidents
- decreased motivation or productivity
- decreased morale
- complaints of poor customer service

Although one of the items listed above might not indicate there is a bully in the office, more than one is certainly worthy of attention.

Chapter VI – What Is It Like to Be a Victim of Bullying?

To be any type of victim to abuse is traumatic. And like anyone who has suffered trauma the emotional repercussions can extend from helplessness, to powerlessness, to mood disorders, to behavior disorders, to suicide. Being bullied is not an insignificant matter. It should always be taken seriously by those who hear about it, witness it, and experience it.

Victims of bullying suffer the following symptoms:

- increased absenteeism
- increased stress in being able to complete tasks
- increased accidents on and off the job
- decreased motivation or productivity
- decreased morale
- receive complaints of poor work performance
- anger, unexplained or explained
- frustration and helplessness
- increased sense of vulnerability
- loss of confidence
- inability to sleep
- loss of appetite
- stomach cramps
- headaches
- confusion about why such a 'little' thing bothers them
- self-doubt
- powerlessness
- hopelessness
- suicidal ideation or attempt
- depression

- anxiety
- substance abuse

Although supervisors are not counselors, if these symptoms persist, the employee ought to be recommended for EAP counseling. EAP counseling has the added benefit of being linked to whether the troubled employee remains at work or not. Consult your company's policies for sending employees to counseling.

Chapter VII – Sample Documentation Sheet

An employee needs to begin to fill in this form as soon as any incident arises. If a second incident arises then this log is on its way to becoming an important tool in self-defense. It should be taken to an immediate supervisor as soon as it is possible. If a second incident does not arise, then this form should be stashed somewhere in case the bullying starts up at a later point. Best to start right away with documentation–true bullies rarely bully only once.

Name of people involved:

_____

Date	Time	What occurred	Where	Witnesses	Outcome

Include in the Outcome column a note to whom each incident was reported and whether the bully was confronted, or not, and what occurred after that. For instance, how did it change matters? Try not to get too wordy. The more succinct the notes – the easier it is to read. Commentary on why the bully performed a certain act or an interpretation in any way will only bring in confusion. Keep to the facts. (form created by author)

Chapter VIII - What Should an Employee Do When Bullied in the Workplace?

Every victim should be prepared with a filled in Documentation Sheet, such as the one provided in Chapter VII, when meeting with a supervisor. Facts leave little room for debate.

Always consult with a company hierarchical chart before going to a supervisor. It is imperative to keep to the chain of command. Do not go to a supervisor's supervisor unless the immediate supervisor has been spoken to first and shown the Documentation Sheet. Make sure to also include those meetings on the Documentation Sheet. That being said, there are basically two reasons why companies allow an employee to skip the chain of command:

1. if an employee suspects that his immediate supervisor will retaliate against him in either passive/aggressive behavior or overt actions, and

2. if it is the employee's supervisor who is the bully.

As I said in the beginning of this manual, there is no law on the books for bullying in the workplace so find out what the company's policy is on any other type of harassment and follow that procedure. That way, there can be no dismissal of the bullying complaint because company policy was not followed. Most companies have actual Incident Reports which can be filled out in addition to the Documentation Sheet. Victims should always make a copy of any and all papers that are handed over to a supervisor. If possible, they shouldn't type any of these forms and reports on the

company computer. Paperwork should be taken to the victim's home and kept on a personal computer.
All victims can always consult with an outside employment attorney but many companies already come equipped with attorneys in the human relations department. Sometimes supervisors consider being bullied an employee personality problem – be aware of this – even though bullies are likely to be sociopaths, it is the victim that is often blamed for the incidents.

As frustrating as this is, keep the Documentation Sheet and other forms filled out and keep pursuing the issue with those supervisors responsible for the department. Victims are not to blame for bullying. It is not a victim's fault that a sociopath is acting out. This is far from a personality issue. If skipping the chain of command is necessary because the bully is a good friend of a particular supervisor – indicate that detail on the Documentation Sheet. The more facts that are listed on the Documentation Sheet, including the reason why a decision was made to side-step company policy, the better.

Victims should not attempt to try and reason with the bully about how immature and inappropriate his behavior is, even though it might be tempting to appeal to the reasonable side of him. Trust me, on this issue, there is no reasonable side. Think about it. Any adult who bullies is not going to be rational. Bullying behavior stems from a personal and deep-rooted psychological issue.

I cannot say this strongly enough: when bullying behavior occurs within the confines of company life, the problem belongs to the management of that company. Victims should take this matter to their immediate supervisors, without hesitation.

[20]

When presenting the case against a bullying work environment, a victim should evince an expectation that the supervisor be responsible for providing a non-hostile work environment. Make a clear, concise, and steady case to the supervisor and ask that this matter be addressed within a certain time frame, possibly within a week. Once a bully brings chaos, anger, and ill health to an employee's work and personal life, the job becomes a hostile environment. Hostile work environments are unsafe work environments and problems can escalate quickly. As stated above, victims begin to have many psychological symptoms from abuse. Abusive stress in the workplace should be taken as seriously as any other health issue.

When meeting with a supervisor it is important to stay calm even though the topic is distressful. This does not mean that a victim can't cry or show emotion. After all, victims are in pain. It does mean, however, that it is important to stay focused on the facts and not get hysterical. After all, supervisors need to get the facts and should know that the victim is scared. But they usually don't have time nor is it their place to sift through high emotions. Supervisors are not counselors even though compassion and empathy is required to be a caring supervisor. So, victims should keep to the topic and not start complaining about the overall office temperament or mood. This will simply diffuse the case. By focusing on the facts on The Documentation Sheet a victim can better keep his mind focused.

Briefly, here is what victims of bullying should keep in mind when addressing a supervisor:

1. present exact documentation – brief and to the point,

2. ask for a deadline for when the supervisor will address the problem,

3. do not take the bully's behavior personally. Bullies enjoy it when they get other people upset and reactive. Don't give a bully that power. Victims should keep control over their minds and moods as best they can,

4. victims should be careful to not be persuaded by bullies and inexperienced supervisors to deny the problem. Bullies are predictable. Documenting keeps tally of the effects of their behavior,

5. stay focused on the work hired to do. Victims suffer enough; they shouldn't have to deal with poor evaluations too,

6. always be polite, assertive, and confer with bullies on work issues only. Then get the hell out of their space,

7. hostile situations won't change just because a victim wishes it. Keep the supervisor informed and in the loop of what is infringing on work assignments and co-workers, and

8. never be alone with the bully. Go ahead and miss elevators and whatever other situation has no witnesses.

Review the list in Chapter III and don't dismiss any reactions, physical, emotional, or otherwise. Bullies have a way of getting in the mind of a victim so that they go everywhere with them. Don't let this happen. Keep it at work, knowing that the bully is management's problem.

If the bully enters the personal life of a victim, comes to their home, threatens their family – DO NOT HESITATE TO DIAL 911 AND TAKE THEM TO COURT AND GET AN ORDER OF PROTECTION. Stressful – of course, but necessary. Bullies are used to lives that are stressful and chaotic so they don't have any objection when they bring that chaos into the lives of others. They thrive on it. Victims shouldn't let them thrive in their lives too.

Victims should get counseling, other support, and whatever it takes to get the bully off their backs. Do not try to solicit understanding from the bully about his abuse. It won't happen. Most victims have no other experience with sociopaths or narcissistic personality disorder types so their minds can't wrap around the mental illness of a bully. Not every bully is as severe as this statement but it doesn't matter – they aren't far from it. It is not a victim's job to diagnose them; it is a victim's job to avoid and protect themselves. Period!

Chapter IX - The Responsibility of the Supervisor

Each supervisor must take bullying seriously and must notify the next level of supervisor on the chain of command. Repercussions for companies can be severe should an employee hire a personal employment attorney to handle the case. Not to mention the disastrous outcome for liability if an employee gets hurt or murdered. Even though bullying falls into that grey area of *illegal* discrimination, it doesn't mean other forms of hostility in the workplace should be ignored. Companies can still be sued for failing to prevent a hostile work environment. Law suits cost everyone involved. They are stressful, expensive, and a nuisance. And in companies where there is already a built-in legal counsel, policies and procedures for behavior, law suits against the prevention of a hostile work environment matter is needless.

When meeting with an employee with a complaint about bullying, the following items should be asked of the employee. Does he experience any of the following:

- anxiety about coming to work,
- taking increased tension home to the family,
- an inability to concentrate both at home and at work,
- low morale – doesn't feel like performing to optimum level,
- difficulty with certain employees,
- decreased inability to cope with the stress of the job,
- lack of sleep,
- increased use of addictive substances, or
- increased health problems?

Supervisors might want to assess their departments occasionally to keep up with problems. If any of the following are happening, it is possible there is a bully causing some interpersonal problems. It is certainly worth investigating. Victims don't always feel safe enough to go to supervisors. They often just quit. But an alert supervisor can get a problem solved before negative repercussions arise. Look for the following:

- increased absenteeism,
- increased turnover of staff,
- increased stress in getting staff to respond to work projects or supervisor requests,
- increased costs either due to lack of productivity or increased EAP counseling, sessions
- increased accidents,
- decreased motivation or productivity,
- decreased morale, or
- complaints of poor customer service.

Supervisors should also keep a documentation sheet of actions they took to search out, confront, and remediate the situation. If a bullying problem is presented to counsel, the supervisor will be prepared with documentation of their own. It is the supervisor's job to maintain a non-hostile work environment for his staff. A notice similar to the one below would serve companies well to be posted in viewing areas, on bulletin boards, and presented in hiring sessions:

> *We at (name of company) consider bullying in the workplace unacceptable behavior and such behavior will not be tolerated under any circumstance. (You can list here the behaviors mentioned in Chapter III).*

[25]

Workplace behavior is behavior that harms, intimidates, offends, degrades, and humiliates employees, embarrasses them in front of other employees, clients, and customers. Workplace bullying may cause the loss of trained and talented staff, reduce their productiveness, morale, and create legal problems for all involved.

Our company believes all employees should be able to work in a friendly environment free of bullying which also includes the management staff. Our company has a grievance and investigation policy for such behavior. Any reports will be met with a tone of seriousness, lack of retaliation, and quick response to resolve the problem in the most efficient manner.

Our company encourages all employees, including managers, to report any and all workplace bullying without any need to fear of retaliation.

Disciplinary action will be taken against any employee who bullies an employee of this company. Discipline may involve a warning, transfer, counseling, demotion, or dismissal – depending upon the situation. If you are a victim of bullying or have witnessed such behavior, please contact:

Name_____

Department _____

Phone number _____

(adapted from http://www.northeastern.edu/securenu/?p=1995)

[26]

There are four different levels of incidents about bullying that supervisors need to be aware of. Each one can be disruptive and bring chaos to company departments:

1. A single unprofessional incident – this is a one-time incident that can be easily resolved with a meeting and open discussion – parties need to make amends – no disciplinary action is usually required. Supervisors should still document this event in case it continues. Give a verbal warning that this problem should cease.
2. An apparently forming pattern – when a second event takes place there should be another meeting with documentation and a notice for each party to sign that the behavior will not occur again. Written warning.
3. A pattern that persists – supervisors should have a meeting to discuss disciplinary action with time lines for when behaviors are expected to change. Again, a written notice should be signed. Possible transfers to another department might be warranted. A consult with higher authorities in the company need to occur.
4. An escalated pattern with no changes or signs of diminishing disruptive behavior - termination of the injuring party.

Note that for each level of disruption, different disciplinary actions are warranted.

If supervisors meet with the bully separate from the victim, the victim should be informed about such meetings. Any outcomes that arise within the meeting can certainly be held in confidence – as is the case with other harassment issues.

By informing the victim that the supervisors are working on the issue, the victim can relax in knowing that there is:

1. help from his supervisor to support and protect him, and
2. there is no need to seek legal assistance or take the problem out of the company.

Victims of bullying should also be asked to notify the supervisor immediately if the problem persists and to continue filling out the Documentation Sheet.

Supervisors should not send their distressed employees back to their desks to either ignore or handle the situation on their own. This will only delay the handling of the problem and might make matters worse and more dangerous. The message supervisors ought to give employees who are victims of bullying is that management will take their incident seriously and will get back to them within a certain period of time – no longer than 30 days for an outcome but within the week for contact with the bully. Safety issues ought not to be given a month to be confronted even though finding solutions might take longer. **Also to push the bullying problem too far into the future before managers meet about the problem will only serve to give the victim employee the message that management is not taking the incident seriously.**

Supervisors certainly don't want the victim employee to try to take matters into their own hands with a person who is irrational, immature, and inappropriate enough to use bullying as a tactic in the workplace. This can set up a dangerous situation.

Supervisors have the right to make a bully's continued employment conditional upon counseling help. Because of the profile of bullies I suggest supervisors confront bullies when two supervisors are present, perhaps ask the security guard to stay nearby, or conduct the meeting in an EAP counselor's office. And it is wise to always direct them to the EAP counseling office. That is one of the terrific benefits of having an EAP.

Proceed with caution when approaching and meeting with a persistent bully. The emphasis should be put on keeping *everyone* safe not just the victim. Because of the mental health issues bullies act out, they should never be made to feel helpless or powerless in meetings. Allow bullies to speak their minds, keep the meeting calm and focused on the **behavior** that is not tolerated, not the personal attributes of the **person**. Let the bully know exactly what is required. Give suggestions for how to handle their distress because they too could be reacting to some problem that is legitimate. But when all is said and done, the one thing remains, the management team needs to make it clear that bullying must stop and will not be tolerated. **The final word for supervisors is: take bullying in the workplace seriously and do not tolerate it and always give some form of disciplinary action even if it is EAP counseling.**

It is in the best interest of everyone involved for the supervisor to be prepared with an agreement for the bully to sign making him aware of the behavior that will not be tolerated and how much time is reasonable for him to make the changes that is required. Be specific. Remember, bullies do not believe that they are doing anything inappropriate. For the most part, they are acting out something that seems *right* to them and is quite familiar, be it childhood drama or some other cause of PTSD that they believe they have a right to act out. They do not see it as acting out as others do. To them it is their paradigm of justice. Bullying behavior is how the bully feels powerful. This belief distortion should be worked out in an EAP counseling session.

Resources

The best way to take action on this is to start a petition and ask others to sign it. Go to:
www.Change.org.

Here are some sites to check out:

http://www.bullyonline.org/workbully/serial.htm

www.worksafe.wa.gov.au/newsite/worksafe/media/Guide_bullying_emplo.pdf

http://www.bullyonline.org/workbully/survivor.htm

http://educate.crisisprevention.com/Workplace-Bullying.html?code=ITG024OBR&src=Pay-Per-Click&gclid=CLHspvHQu7cCFS3l7Aod0TIAhQ

http://www.foxnews.com/health/2013/04/25/how-to-cope-with-bullying-in-workplace/

http://www.workplacebullying.org/

http://bullyinglte.wordpress.com/2010/05/21/a-poem-on-workplace-bullying/

http://www.bullyonline.org/workbully/survivor.htm

http://www.bullyonline.org/cases/index.htm

http://www.eeoc.gov/laws/types/

http://portal.hud.gov/hudportal/HUD

http://portal.hud.gov/hudportal/HUD?src=/about/hud_history

www.workplacebullying.org/2010/09/30/workplace-bullying

www.ccohs.ca/oshanswers/psychological/bullying.html

www.fredlaw.com/articles/employment/empl

http://www.northeastern.edu/securenu/?p=1995

About the Author

Jan Marquart LCSW

Jan Marquart is a licensed clinical social worker, educator, author, and dynamic motivational speaker. She facilitates workshops in the workplace on a variety of topics, including stress management, communication, harassment, job burnout, and how to deal with a bully in the workplace. Jan currently has a private practice, the heart of which is directed towards structural and psychodynamic/cognitive behavioral functions. Her specialty is corporate and family systems.

Jan is also an author, CEO and Founder of About the Author Network. All her books can be found on her site: www.JanMarquart.com.

www.JanMarquart.com
512 795 0074
jan_marquart@yahoo.com - or -
jan@AboutTheAuthorNetwork.com
www.AboutTheAuthorNetwork.com